HOW TO WRITE YOU BOOK

Book 1 – Let's Get Started

From an Idea...

"the Editor"
Ms. Edi Tor

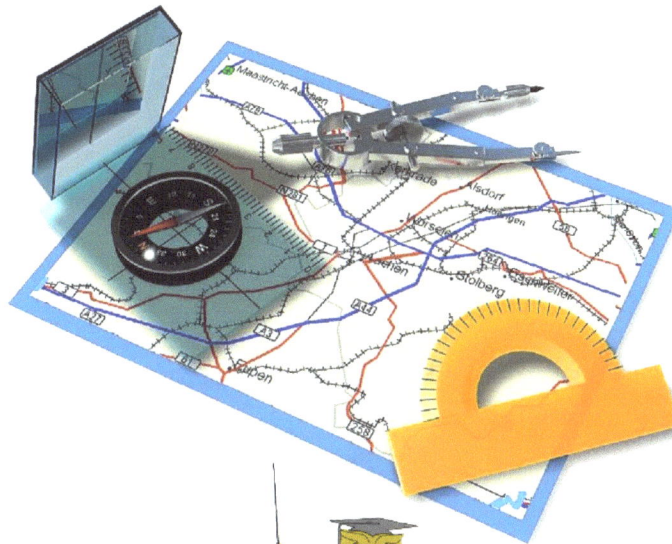

"the Publisher"
Mr. I. M. Publisher

"the Writer"
Ms. Iwanna B. Writer

to your Finished Story

as narrated by
The Three Wise Guides

Bobbi Madry & Francine Barish-Stern

Published By Golden Quill Press
a division of Barish-Stern Ltd.
P O Box 83
Troutville, VA 24175

ISBN 978-0-9847330-19

Cover by Art on Gold, Troutville, Va.
Interior Design by Kenneth A. Bray, Troutville Va.

Printed by CreateSpace, An Amazon.com Company
Available from Amazon.com and other retail outlets
Available from Amazon.com and other online stores
Available from Amazon.com and other book stores
Available from Amazon.com, CreateSpace.com, and other retail outlets
A reference to an Amazon review
Available on Kindle and other devices
Available on Kindle and other retail outlets
Available on Kindle and other book stores
Available on Kindle and online stores

Most people believe they can write a book

But most people don't know how to begin?

Writers need to understand what makes a book a good read!

"the Writer"
Ms. Iwanna B. Writer

"the Editor"
Ms. Edi Tor

"the Publisher"
Mr. I. M. Publisher

INTRODUCTION

"From an Idea...to your Finished Story," as narrated by "The Three Wise Writing Guides," is an interactive journey into the exciting world of writing. On this journey our guides: **the Writer**, Ms. Iwanna B. Writer, **the Editor**, Ms. Edi Tor, and **the Publisher**, Mr. I.M. Publisher, will give tips, information and you can download interactive writing tools designed to help anyone who wants to write. This combined book was developed as a direct result of the authors' years of experience, as published authors, editors and publishers. From our writing workshops and interactive seminars we gained an understanding of writers' specific needs. We concluded that most participants were unable to take their ideas from the seedling stage to the finished story. For the most part, great story ideas would pop-up, then ultimately fizzle, from the task of getting these ideas down on paper. Workshop questionnaires and writing assignments revealed that not only aspiring writers, but also the more experienced could benefit from learning how to properly structure their great ideas into finished stories. Overcoming obstacles by setting realistic goals proved to be helpful in keeping writers on track and motivating them to complete their projects. Once they began to think like in a writing format, the

1

quality of their work improved and they were able to see their writing projects through to completion.

How Will This Book Benefit You?

Whether you're a beginner or an established writer, *"From an Idea...to your Finished Story,"* was designed to meet any writer's needs. Our Three Writing Guides will assist you through the process: prepare you to write, help you get your good ideas down on paper and walk you through revising and editing. They'll stay with you as you finish your work and prepare your manuscript, and then offer advice to those of you with an eye toward publishing. Different people write for different reasons. Whether your reasons are profit, therapy or to see your ideas down on paper, or in print, these Guides want to HELP YOU!

Take this quiz:

... THIS BOOK IS RIGHT FOR ME, IF ...

- ♦ I've ever envisioned writing a book, but didn't know where to start — so I didn't start.

- ♦ I've ever sat down to write and got stalled — so I never continued.

- ♦ I've ever written my ideas down on paper, but couldn't turn them into a story.

- ♦ I've ever finished a writing project, and then didn't know what to do with it.

- ♦ I've ever finished my writing project and had people tell me it would be the next best seller, but it wasn't.

- I've ever sent my work to publishers and received rejections.

- I've received rejections that upset me, and I eventually stopped sending out my work.

- I've put my work in a bottom drawer; believing I would take it out someday — but didn't.

  - I am nodding, "..that's happened to me," then

Today is YOUR "Writer's Birth Day"

and the Wise Guides have a SPECIAL Gift for You... **This Book!**

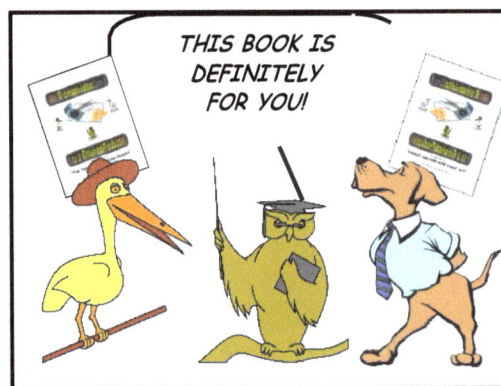

Understanding your writing needs, the authors have chosen the

Three Wise Writing Guides to travel with you on your writing journey.

Our Guides will:

- Pinpoint important information to help you map out your voyage

- Highlight details to be aware of to ensure a completed journey

3

- Give you writing assignments to help you perfect your skills and enable you to maneuver around the bumps in the road

- Provide helpful hints and detours to take when you hit writer's roadblocks

- Urge you on with a suitcase packed full of helpful resources

The Wise Guides will provide you with maps you'll need to travel to your writing destination and ensure that you have a safe, completed journey. Best of all they will be your Passenger and Navigator as you Journey together —

"From an Idea... to your Finished Story."

To get the most out of your journey, use the examples you'll find throughout the book to give you a better understanding of the writing topics. You will also be prompted to "DO IT NOW" at various points. We suggest you use these areas to personalize your writing. As an added bonus, Golden Quill Press Travel Company has provided Extra Bonus Travel Forms that correspond to each Travel Map; at the back of each chapter. These forms will reinforce the information in each chapter and give you an additional opportunity to develop your story. If you've already written your story, then you can use all of these points for editing and revising. We want to emphasize, whether you're a novice or an experienced writer, this book has been designed to provide a step-by-step approach to writing and completing your story. Our guides were created from our experiences and as a way to make this a fun journey that will spur you on to travel

"From an Idea... to your Finished Story."

4

Look for Road Signs to Help You on Your Journey

These signs have been designed to ensure you don't get lost. They'll keep you pointed in the right direction and on the right roads during every aspect of your writing trip.

Trip Signs: These Writing Map Signs will identify each new chapter of your journey as a color coordinated Writing Map. Think of these signs as the Welcome Sign you see when entering a new state that you must pass through to get to your final destination. Each sign will also correspond to the Travel Forms at the back of each chapter.

DO IT NOW! **Map Sign:** This sign will alert you to ATTRACTIONS worth stopping at. Visiting will help to reinforce chapter information.

Travel Folders: Throughout this book you'll be prompted to create folders. We suggest setting up physical File Folders as well as computer files. The Forms are divided into Example and Exercise. A Feature of The Examples is that they follow an actual book, Golden Quill Press' "Code 47 to BREV Force."

Suitcase: Finally we have to pack for the voyage— So use this SUITCASE to Pack all materials, supplies, file folders, extra forms and any other materials you will need to travel *"From an Idea...to your Finished Story."* Each chapter review will tell you what to put in your suitcase. Remember Your Suitcase is also an organizer file. It should contain everything you'll need and can be a physical file and a computer file.

Pit Stops: This book also offers interactive Service Stations placed strategically along your route to assist you in making those necessary pit stops. You will find: Web Support — E-mail Tech Support — Forums — and Benefits all designed to help you get back on the road. Look for these Road Signs when you need that pit stop—

We also suggest that whenever you want to remember some point we've made or in order to trigger something specific you want to remember when you begin writing, you create a **Map Pin**. Your map pin is basically the Map Number, Page Number and Topic. Using **Map Pins will help you easily** locate that information, and get you moving on your voyage.

Travel Kit Form

Travel Forms: At the end of each Chapter you will find this sign that will alert you to additional exercises available by download to any computer. These are FREE and support the information in the Chapter. You may also be prompted to use them along your journey by DO IT NOW!

Writing is hard work— but anything worthwhile is worth working for. But also remember that writing is an art that can be learned; it's not brain surgery. No matter what level of writing skills you possess, by following the techniques laid out in this book, you should be able to see yourself as a writer and achieve your goal of a completed manuscript. We also want you to remember — books can be written in a matter of months— or a matter of years. Some authors take years because they write and then put their work in a drawer for stretches of time. We imagine more good books are in drawers, then have been published. If this describes you, go get your work now and take it out — if you haven't started; commit with us now to get started! If it is a work in progress, commit to stick with it, until it's a finished story!

Think of your writing as embarking on an adventure that is only complete when you reach your writing destination. If you do, you'll have a more positive outlook, and a stronger motivation to finish your work.

It takes confidence and belief in what you're trying to accomplish in order to begin this journey. The Three Wise Writing Guides believe in you; after all, you've taken the first step by using, *"From an Idea...to your Finished Story,"* to help you get started. These experienced guides will lead you on the right roads and provide the knowledge and tools you'll need for a successful trip. The Guides will be with you every step of the way, until your journey is completed. Ask any author what it feels like to finish their story and believe they have made it their best. That's the feeling we want you to experience.

Success doesn't necessarily happen overnight. Writing journeys can be filled with unexpected delays, road blocks, detours and pitfalls. Just believe that when you finally reach your destination and have a finished work—it will all have been worthwhile! So let's get the right vehicle, pack everything you need, including your Travel Maps, and follow The Three Writing Guides down the Golden Quill Roads to Your Finished Story!

BON VOYAGE !!!

Your writing journey will begin with ideas and tips to help you get started toward achieving your writing goals

"the Writer"
Ms. Iwanna B. Writer

Driving You to Your Finished Story

Helping You Every Step of Your Journey

"the Editor"
Ms. Edi Tor

"the Publisher"
Mr. I. M. Publisher

Writing Map 1

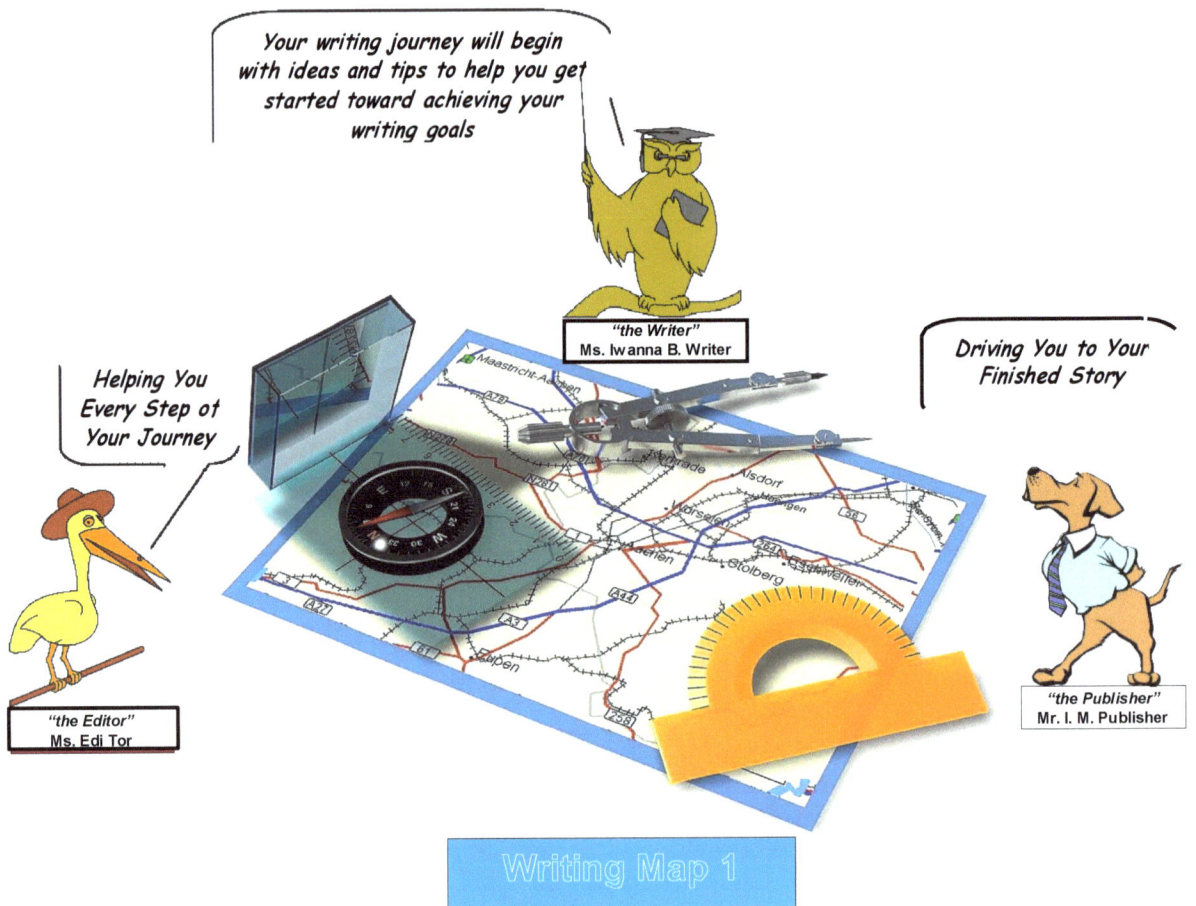

PLANNING YOUR WRITING JOURNEY

Before you begin any journey you must plan:

- ◆ Where you want to go

- ◆ How you will get there

- ◆ What you need to pack

- ◆ What you will do when you get there, etc.

And, like any great trip, having an experienced guide can help you avoid the bumps in the road and make the experience that much better. Ms. Iwanna B. Writer will be assisting you through this phase of your writing trip. Ms. Edi Tor and Mr. I.M. Publisher will also add their comments throughout this stage.

Planning List: Set Your Writing Destination - Have you ever wondered what would've happened if explorers started on their journey without a defined destination? Or, why so many people have started on journey's, braved hardships yet never gave up? All of them believed in their dreams; addressed potential obstacles, anticipated achieving their goals and then off they started down the road, confident of their destination.

Our Guide's Agree and Suggest

Take your great ideas, unfinished works, or writing that you have stashed in a drawer; and let's get started NOW!

First, set your writing destination:

Are you writing for?

Yourself?

Others?

To Publish?

I want to begin my writing journey with a

Book

Short Story/Article

Personal History

Whatever you are writing, once you can identify your destination clearly, your next step will be: get organized, prepare the right tools and establish a designated place to write. Once you have the tool and the place all you need is to plan the time to write.

Use these ideas to get started:

◆ **You Need A Place To Write -** This doesn't have to be a mountain top retreat, or a penthouse suite. Many of our best writers have produced their most outstanding work the kitchen table, park bench or any place they could use pen and paper. Do you have a place to write? If not, you need to find one. It should be secure, quiet and private.

Decide on a location where you will write

Make a "DO NOT DISTURB" sign to put on the door

Set up your files and supplies

Most Importantly — Don't forget to tell your family!

It's very important in achieving your goals that your family understand your commitment and extend their complete support.

◆ **You Need to Choose Your Vehicle For Writing -**

Computer, Typewriter, Tape Recorder, Dictation or Longhand

Some of our best literature was, and still is, written in longhand or on clattering typewriters. But in this day and age, if you can use a computer, that might be the vehicle of choice. Computers make it much easier to write, revise and save your work.

11

They can also give you access to the internet for unlimited research and resources. If you've been thinking about a computer, consider it an investment in your writing future. It's important to have an easy-to-use and up-to-date version of word processing software. Microsoft Word is popular for PC's (personal computers) and is considered fairly easy to use. If you do choose a computer our experts want you to remember these important rules that will save you time, aggravation and the possibility of lost work — In addition to saving your work file, you should have some type of back-up system: either a flash drive, CD's or an external back-up, or cloud. Whenever you finish a writing time, **Save** the entire work to that system. Also while you are writing, **SAVE OFTEN!**

If you're going to require lessons to use computer software – it may be too complicated and delay your leaving on your writing journey. So, find the vehicle that best suits your needs or, go back to what has worked for published authors in the past — typewriters or just plain longhand! Remember you can always get your writing computerized later. Time is money and timely topics burn hot and then fizzle out. Don't wait until you are computer savvy to get started writing.

◆ **You Need the Right Writing Tools -** Keeping pads, pens and sharpened pencils around the house, especially by your bed for those late night ideas, works great! Small notebooks in your purse or jacket and post-its in your house, office and car can be a big help for jotting down ideas that come when you least expect them. When placing your

12

post-it's around be sure the family and or co-workers know they're only intended for your writing notes. Don't forget to put those notes in your Travel Folder (see below). And, because you never know when you'll get a flash of inspiration driving in the car, or taking long walks, a small tape recorder is great to save ideas. Don't forget a good dictionary and thesaurus are also essential writing tools. Sometimes just **changing that one word to something more descriptive can greatly enhance**

your work.

◆ **You Need to Set Up Your Travel Folders -** Set up a system of 8½" x 11" file folders (different colors can make this an easy information access system), in which you pack all your ideas, notes and research information. Separate folders keep your work organized and help you sort ideas. These folders should be easily accessible in your writing area. Make it a habit of putting a date on your notes and review the newest ones before each new writing session. If you're using a computer, set up a main folder for your work on your desktop and then create sub-folders for your computer notes within that folder. Example: "From an Idea...to Your Finished Story," is the main folder. Then inside that folder is your main manuscript and sub-folders for your notes. We suggest in addition to computer folders you also have manila file folders, (as described above).

Now that we have everything for our trip the next step is to PACK!

Our Guides Packing List:

Once you've gathered everything on your list, set up your writing area so that it's comfortable and ready for you to begin your writing session.

◆ **You Need Time to Write -** It would be ideal to be able to write full time, but many writers don't have that luxury. Try to work on your schedule; allowing time for job and family – to find your writing time. As we've suggested, having family support can play a big role in achieving your writing destination.

Managing your writing time is also taking control of your life. Twenty-four hours seems like a lot of time to some people; little time to others. It's all a matter of how you manage your activities and how you view priorities. The Three Wise Guides use the motto: "**Save time by ditching the clutter."** Have on hand only the items you need. Have a place for everything and everything in its place.

Try to analyze your day and see where you have time-wasting activities**.**
Keep a record of what you do each day for an entire week to help you see where your time is spent. When your daily schedule involves a number of activities, you will need to find the best time to write: Many daily activities can't be changed, but if you really want time to write, you must find the time— and you will! It's not so much a matter of when you write, but that you write as often and as much as possible. One of the main reasons is to help you retain your continuity of thought. If you do not have a structured writing schedule the task of continuing thoughts from previous writing sessions will be much

Writing Map 1 **PACKING LIST** Form
Fill in your writing supplies
When Completed store in your Travel Folder

more difficult.

 The WRITING APPOINTMENT CALENDAR is available at the back of the   chapter to help you set the best times for writing. There's a saying: "If you don't know where you're   going, that's where you'll go—nowhere," so, use this Calendar to follow   your course and keep you on the right writing track to finishing your work. Remember: *If you search for it—you will find it,* and in this case time is of the essence. Congratulate yourself when you find extra time and feel good about that writing session time. If   you feel guilty, it will show in your work—so, just find another time. Plan your writing time, the same way you make any important commitment, except this one is with yourself. You wouldn't cancel an appointment that's important to your future, so be sure to

adhere to these times. Look at your schedule today and commit to a
regular time to write. Start with small steps you can handle; even if it's just a brief amount of time. Writing at regular intervals is more important at first than how long each session lasts. Once you get started you'll find the time to write on a regular basis.

Writers generally think they can create the perfect story in less time than it took to create the world. We must think realistically and plan to write regularly!

 Most of us have the best intentions -- I will go to the gym today, I will take a walk-- I will write-- but most times if we don't set that time aside, the end of the day comes and you're amazed that you didn't get any of these things done. We've learned from our writing seminars that when life happens, writing time can be the first to go. But,   when we had our writers establish set times and prioritize their activities, they succeeded in not only   finding the time, but becoming disciplined enough to make the time.

Set that appointment and don't forget to mark it in your daily planner or wherever you keep track of appointments.

Then, use the Appointment Calendar and mark every time you have a writing session, how long it lasted and what you accomplished.

Writing Map 1 **APPOINTMENT CALENDAR** Form

Fill out the information as shown in the example.
When Completed store in your Travel Folder

Post it prominently, where it will be visible to you, daily.

Don't Forget to go over all your Actual Writing Times at the end of each week to review your accomplishments and use the information as a guide to set your schedule for the following week. Then, put the finished form in Your Writing Appointments Folder for future reference.

Monday	Time		Appointment Assignment	Time		Actually Completed
	From	To		From	To	
June 5 / 06	7:30 PM	11:00 PM	*Work On Main Character Development* EXAMPLE	8:00 PM	10:30 PM	*Completed Main Character & Her Family – 5 Characters – Put in File*

◆ **You Need to Set Priorities** - Creative writers often have many good ideas, but don't take time to sort them out. Sometimes those ideas are like a traveler without a map or a tapestry with threads going in all directions. Being disciplined helps you to focus on the big picture—your finished work. It's best to concentrate on only one writing project now and give yourself a reasonable deadline. Procrastination is the writer's greatest enemy! If you set positive and realistic goals, you will have a better chance of succeeding. Decide what you want to accomplish first; then begin working toward completing that writing project.

In order to keep you on track we recommend establishing an anticipated completion date and writing that date at the bottom of each of your Appointment Calendars. Use that date to review your accomplishments and to try and set a realistic completion date.

Make a sign to display in your writing space to remind you of the goal you are working toward!

My Writing Project Is:
_____
I Am Beginning My Writing Journey on
_____
Start Date
I Will Review My Writing Project on
_____
6 months from Start Date

◆ **You Need to Have Purpose -** Why do you want to write? This is a question only you can answer.

The following list was compiled from a questionnaire used in a writer's workshop that asked writers of various ages, occupations and lifestyles: "Why do you want to write?" Their answers may help you gain more insight into your own reasons for writing.

When reading their answers, decide what your reasons are to write

I want to write because:

- I have a passion for reading good literature and writing gives me an opportunity to see my ideas come alive on the page.

- I find writing helps me to express my inner feelings about life and the world around me.

- I have a story I feel needs to be told and I am strongly motivated to write.

- Writing is my life. I find it therapeutic.

- I believe everyone has a story to tell and I'd like to write my story.

- I would like to become a published author. Not so much for fame or fortune (though that would be nice), but to share my knowledge and experiences with others.

- I want to become a published author for the money and fame.

- Writing is a creative activity I enjoy.

- Writing well is an asset in my career. Companies today are looking for applicants that have good communication skills. Writing skills top the list.

Take a moment, re-read the above reasons for writing and then compose your "Travel Statement" and post it where you write to remind you and encourage you on!

Now that we understand why you want to write let's see what skills you have and what you need to work on.

◆ **You Need to Chart Your Strengths and Weaknesses** - The purpose of charting is to identify your strongest skills and positive personal qualities. Knowing these can help you accomplish your task of finishing the work you start.

In every workshop we've conducted, procrastination was the one problem most writers agreed they needed to overcome. They got started okay, but then let everything else get in the way. Having an understanding of these road blocks will help you when "life happens." Remember too, that sometimes it's easier to put your writing away than it is to work through a problem. So you need to be prepared.

◆ **Personal Evaluation Chart** - Divide a piece of paper in half. On the left List **(+) POSITIVE STRONG POINTS qualities**, skills and accomplishments and On the Right List **(–) NEGATIVE WEAK POINTS obstacles** you allow to deter you and get in your way to reaching your writing goals.

BE VERY HONEST! You are the only one who has to see this list, but if you do it right it will help you when you need it most!

Example: If you were discouraged because of writer's block and decided to stop writing (Negative Trait) Your (Positive) Strong Determination and commitment would see you through!

◆ **You Need to Use the Chart to Develop Your Right Writing Course -**

Writing is an art and craft that is easy for some and difficult for others. Use the chart to increase your Positive traits. Remember: "Patience, Practice and Persistence! Don't let Writing No's such as, "I'm tired, I can't think of anything, I'm probably wasting my time…." and the like, contribute to your downfall. Learn to Use The Power of Your Positive Points to Overcome your Negative Ones. Think of situations in advance that might stop you from writing and plan a course of action when something happens to interfere with your writing!

TRIP REVIEW

MAP DIRECTIONS

Every Successful Journey Begins With Planning
Writers Succeed One Mile At A Time
Sticking To Road Maps Will Get You To Your Final Destination
New Roads Can Offer New Ideas
Travel Instructions — Did You?
Stake out your Place to Write & Discuss Writing With Your Family
Obtain Tools and Equipment for Your Writing Needs
Design a Writing Appointment Schedule to Keep You on Track
Post it Prominently Where You Will see It
and Put it in Your

Decide on an Anticipated Completion Date

OUR GUIDES
POINT YOU IN THE RIGHT DIRECTION

Being well prepared will help you to stay on track!

Get used to using a Dictionary and a Thesaurus. They are wonderful tools!

CONGRATUATIONS!! We are all 100% behind your efforts!

◀ **NOTE** ▶

New technologies are constantly presenting exciting challenges for writers. Even when you feel confident of your writing abilities, it's always important to keep your eye on ways to improve your skills and present the best finished product possible.

Reading published authors will help you develop better skills.

WRITING APPOINTMENT CALENDAR

Writing Map 1						Travel Kit Form
Monday *June 5 / 06*	**Time** From | To *7:30* *PM* | *11:00* *PM*		**Appointment Assignment** *Work On Main Character* *Development* **EXAMPLE**	**Time** From | To *8:00* *PM* | *10:30* *PM*		**Actually Completed** *Completed Main Character &* *Her Family - 5 Characters -* *Put in File*

☐ ☐☐☐☐ APP☐☐☐ME☐☐☐ALE☐☐A☐ ☐ ☐E

Day	Time From	Time To	Appointment Assignment	Time From	Time To	Actually Completed
Sunday						
Monday						
Tuesday						
Wednesday						
Thursday						
Friday						
Saturday						

Go Over all your Actual Writing Sessions at the end of the week to review your writing times and use the information as a guide to set your schedule for the following week. Then put this form in Your Writing Appointments Folder for future reference.

If Additional Space is required permission is given to copy this form

The Guides Packing List :

☐   Pens (Include a RED Pen & Highlighters)   ☐ Pencils with Erasers

☐   Post-it's (Get a STAND OUT Color or Florescent, but ☐ Pencil Sharpener

not too dark so you can't read what you write BRIGHT YEL- ☐ Pads

LOW may work)   ☐ Notebook

☐   Manila Folders (Colors are preferable)   ☐ Dictionary

☐   8.5 11 White Paper   ☐ Thesaurus

☐   Small Tape Recorder &Tapes   ☐ Timer

☐   Computer Floppy Disks and/or CD's (depending upon your ☐ Do Not Disturb Sign

system needs)   ☐ Your Writing Goal Sign

OTHER: -   _____   _____

◆   _____   _____   _____

◆   _____   _____   _____

◆   _____   _____   _____

◆   _____   _____   _____

◆   _____   _____   _____

◆   _____   _____   _____

◆   _____   _____   _____

◆   _____   _____   _____

◆   _____   _____   _____

◆   _____   _____   _____

If Additional Space is required permission is given to copy this form

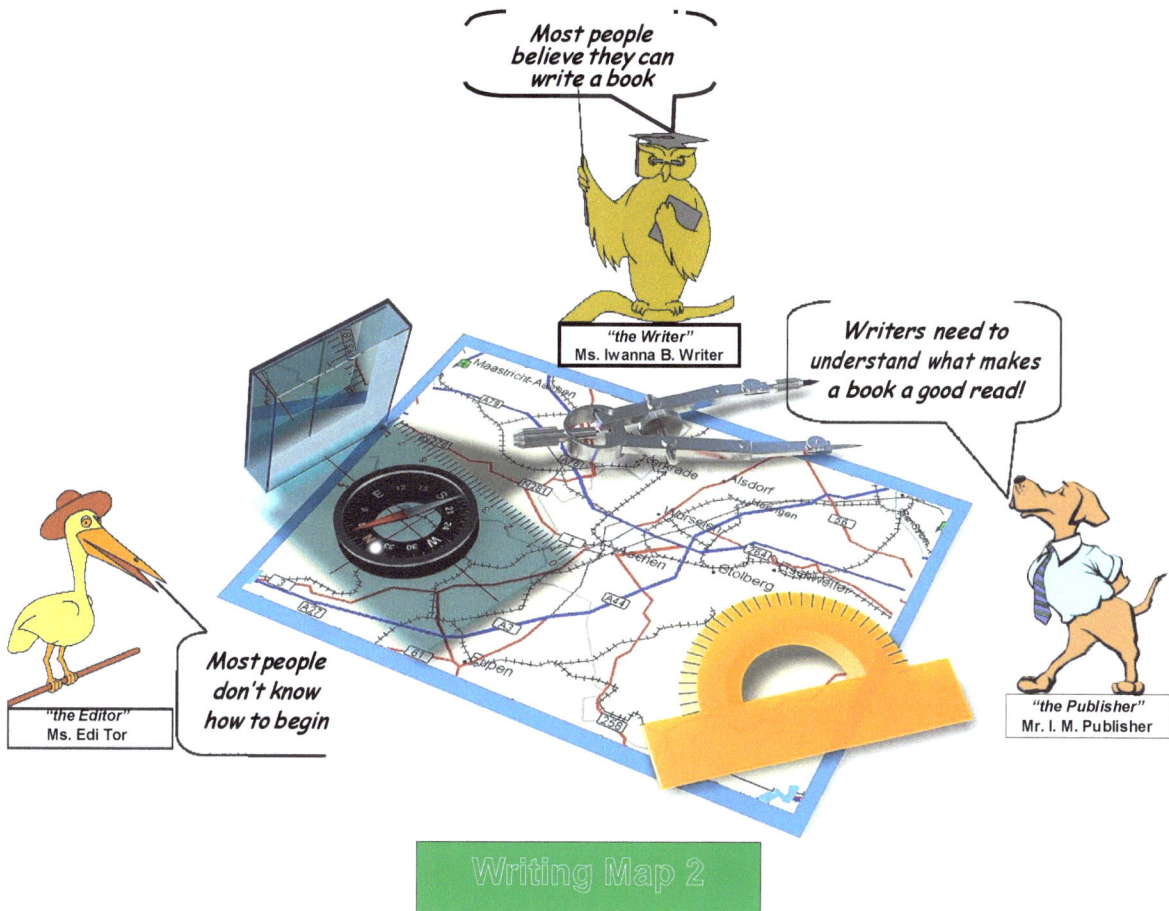

"the Writer"
Ms. Iwanna B. Writer

Most people
believe they can
write a book

Writers need to
understand what makes
a book a good read!

Most people
don't know
how to begin

"the Editor"
Ms. Edi Tor

"the Publisher"
Mr. I. M. Publisher

Writing Map 2

PREPARING TO WRITE

Now that you've settled on a place to write and have gotten all necessary materials gathered into your writing suitcase, it's time to begin formulating story ideas. Whether you're writing a short story, or a novel, the process is essentially the same. You need to begin at the beginning with an idea. Writers sometimes want to start with a Title and they spend a great deal of time and effort deciding on one. But, as you will learn, titles can change, so don't be too concerned with the Title at this point! Just choose a temporary title that you feel suits your story.

How do you begin to gather your story ideas? Many ideas for stories

are derived from personal experiences. People tend to want to tell about their own life or loved ones. Some people write strictly from imagination; building a concept, then expanding on it. Others get ideas from: headlines, visiting or reading about places and events, but where ever your ideas come from, you need to have a clear understanding of your idea before you begin writing. In Writing Map 1 you began your writing journey; now let's continue down the road to getting you, *"From an idea... to your Finished Story."*

The Right Road is this WAY

The best way to get on the Right Road to Writing is to ask for Directions!

So, Ask Questions!

My Writing Idea is about:

My Life

Someone Else's Life

A Story I will conceive

History: People, Places or Events

Real or Conceived

Decide Whether Your Story is Fiction Or Non – Fiction

Fiction: invented, imaginary stories, made up by the author not restricted to fact

Non-Fiction: stories based on fact, rather than the imagination

Decide On A Format

Format is the writing plan for constructing your story. This applies to a short story, novella or a novel.

Short story: shorter than a novel, normally dealing with fewer characters and less action – generally between 7,000 and 10,000 words, but can be fewer. Science Fiction is generally less than 7,500 words.

Novella: a short novel, more than 7,500 but fewer than 40,000 words.

Novel: much longer than the short story, generally, 40,000 words or more. This format enables the writer to develop a wider range of characters and a much more complex plot.

Mapping out a Premise

The premise of a story is a statement or assertion on which your story is based and is the seed from which your story will grow. So how do you decide on your premise? Think of your premise as a descriptive explanation of your idea. Instead of saying, I'm writing about my life, say, I'm writing about being an American growing up in Europe during World War II. You can see we've expanded your idea just by embellishing the

| | Writing Map 2 **IDEA TO OUTLINE** Form

Fill out the information on **#1 and #2 IDEA / PREMISE**
When Completed store in your Travel Folder | |

statement.

The Five "W's" Structuring Formula

As any reporter will tell you there's a formula for writing an outline for a good story and we suggest using the same formula for your writing. When structuring a story, the five "W's" formula can help you keep organized.

The five "W's" are:

- Who -   Who is the story about?

- What - What happened?

- Where - Where did it happen?

- When - When did it happen?

- Why -   Why did it happen?

- *Note: How did it happen? *(we also add How)

Whether you're a beginning novelist or an experienced writer, the five "W's" formula is especially helpful to any writer as a structuring guide. The "W's" need not be in the order shown here, but a well told story needs to include each point.

Get your Writing Map 2 **IDEA TO OUTLINE** Form
from your Travel Folder

Add #3 - the 5W's that pertain to your story
When Completed store in your Travel Folder

The Outline Highway Takes Your Ideas Out For A Spin

One of the best ways to plan a story is to take your premise and your 5 W's and make a list or outline of the most important points you want to cover. An outline helps you to see your story take shape. You might think it's easier to just sit down at the computer or with a pen and blank paper and let your story flow.

But your writer and editor guides suggest:

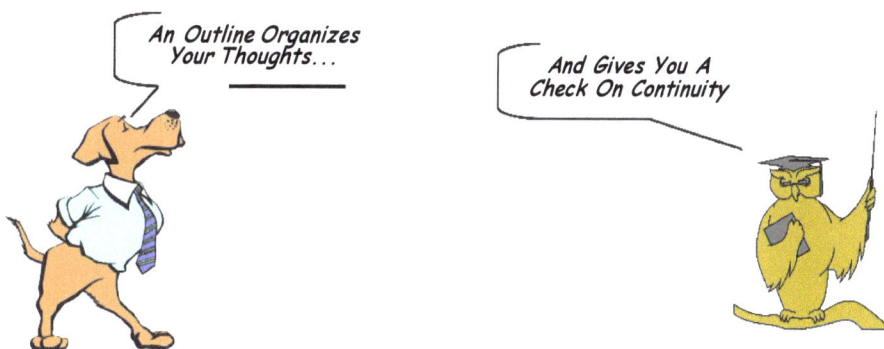

An Outline Organizes Your Thoughts...

And Gives You A Check On Continuity

An outline will help you organize your story and keep an accurate flow, while helping you tie up loose ends. A good outline makes your story come full circle with a beginning, middle, and an end.

Think of the outline as the skeleton of a story (the basic or rough concept) which you then add flesh to with additional details. In our workshops we demonstrate "fleshing" by drawing a skeleton. Then as we add details to the story, such as plot, characters, settings, time periods and much more, the flesh is added as it takes shape over the bones.

REMEMBER This basic working outline helps you to get a clear picture of how to get *from your idea...to your finished story.*

EXAMPLE:

#1 IDEA: Adventurers of a lost Bear.

#2 PREMISE: A priceless bear is missing from the zoo.

#3 THE 5W's:

Who - A priceless white bear cub named Polar

2ⁿᵈ Who - Dr. John Kay, director of the Zoo   **Note**: stories can have many whos for one subject so try and answer the pertinent Who's first

What – Polar the Bear Cub was reported stolen from the Zoo, but was later reported wandering around Ellisville

Where - Ellisville Park Zoo

When - 5 a.m. Tuesday May 15

Why - An investigation is underway. Police Chief Bill Norton said bear knapping had not been ruled out, because the bear is an endangered species and is priceless

How – The door was found open

#4 OUTLINE:

Dr. John Kay, director of the Ellisville Park Zoo, reported that a bear named Polar; a priceless cub, listed on the endangered species list, had disappeared from the zoo early Tuesday morning. The bear's attendant found the door of the steel-wire cage open and officials couldn't rule out bear-knapping. When questioned the zoo attendant, however, swore he didn't leave the door unlatched. Later reports stated the bear was wandering on the highway north of Ellisville, without the so called, "knapper." The bear was eventually found at the "Old Honey Mill," and was returned to the zoo unharmed. Police

Chief, Bill Norton said officials told him Polar, now weighed considerably more than when he went AWOL. Everyone concluded the bear had a fine time. A last   minute note to this story stated that the Honey Mill has submitted a bill to the zoo for $900.00, as the mill was left totally devoid of any honey after Polar's visit.

 This basic outline can now be expanded as you add more details

If you have any questions about outlining, you can e-mail tech support

at: info@goldenquillpress.com - subject: How To Write Book 1- outlining

Writing Map 2 **IDEA TO OUTLINE** Form

Add #4 - your OUTLINE to your form
When Completed store in your Travel Folder

For information regarding Writing Maps or Forms Email:

info@goldenquillpress.com SUBJECT Maps/Forms

TRIP REVIEW

Map Directions

A Good Premise Is A Write Sturdy Foundation

5 W's Formula Help You Get From Who To Where & When To How

Cover Your Skeleton By Fleshing Out The Details

Non-Fiction Or Fiction - Different As Driving On City Streets Or Taking The Highway

Travel Instructions — Did You?

Fill in your Road Sign: Ideas, Fiction or Non-Fiction, Format
Decide on your Premise
Go over the 5 W's for your story
Write your Basic Outline
Now put the form in your Ideas File in your

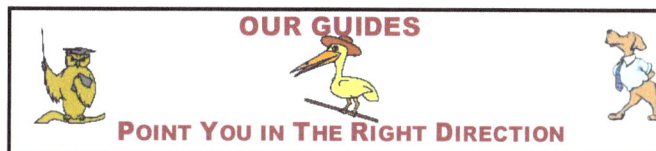

OUR GUIDES

POINT YOU IN THE RIGHT DIRECTION

Properly Gather Your Ideas So You Won't Sound Like A Bird Brain...OOPS!

The 5 W's will prevent your editor - from asking WHO??? (sorry owl)

NOW, You've Really Begun- ARF!

EXAMPLE:	YOUR OUTLINE:
#1 IDEA: Imagined Computer Virus/Super Heroes	**#1 IDEA:** _
#2 PREMISE: Computer Virus goes beyond it's programming to become a sentient being	**#2 PREMISE:** _ _
#3 THE 5W's:	**#3 THE 5W's:**
Who - Controller-computer virus gone awry	*Who* - _____
2nd Who - Cracko– hologram **Note**: stories can have many who's for one subject so try and answer the pertinent Who's first	*2nd Who* - _____ _ _____
What – Controller uses Cracko to recruit college students	*What* – _ _____ _____
Where - Island Falls	*Where* - _____
When - An unknown time	*When* - _____
Why - To become the strongest entity in the world	*Why* - _____
How – By invading all systems and recruiting a human army	*How* - _____
#4 OUTLINE:.	**#4 OUTLINE:** _

EXAMPLE #4 OUTLINE:

A computer virus has grown beyond its original programming and has invaded the small college town of Island Falls. Controller has programmed holograms to do its bidding and to persuade college students to join its ranks.

Scientists Martin and Vivian Kane are recruited to stop Controller. Their children's (Brad and Evie) best friend Jonathan becomes hooked by Controller's forces (hologram Cracko and human helper Sheila) and Brad and Evie strike out on their own to defeat Controller.

From The Authors

CONGRATULATIONS

You Have Made It Through Getting Started on Your Trip!

This is one of the hardest steps… so be proud of your accomplishment and now

On to the Writing Super Highway!

You've earned a rest! Then get back on the road to your finished story with

"How To Write Your Book - From an Idea to Your Finished Story"
Book 2 – Writing Super Highway

Topics In Book 2

Fleshing Out Your Story

Locations, Settings and Time

Getting on the Road to Your Plot

Constructing Your Story

Looking through the Rear View Mirror

So Get Book 2 Now

And Write Your Finished Story!

Golden Quill Press
www.goldenquillpress.com

Words Related to Writing

A

Advance – The amount paid to a writer by a publisher before a book is published. The advance is generally deducted from royalties earned from sales of the finished book.

Agent – A person who represents and acts on behalf of writers.

All rights – The rights contracted to a publisher (magazines, books) to permit the use of a writer's work any time, in any form without paying additional royalties.

Antagonists – A person (characters) who competes with or opposes another. An opponent or adversary.

Assignment – The contract between a writer and editor that confirms dates the writer will complete a project and fees to be paid the writer.

Autobiography – The story of one's own life written or dictated by oneself.

B

Book developer/packager – A business that plans and produces all elements of a book for publishers and producers.

Biography – An account of a person's life written by another.

By-line – The author's name on a published work.

C

Character – A person in a story or play.

Cliché – A trite expression or idea.

Climax – A decisive turning point or action.

Clips – Copies of a writer's work that has been published.

C

Confidant – The person to whom the main character would express undisclosed information the reader needs to know

Conflict – To clash or to be in opposition.

Contemporary – Relating to writing that reflects current trends, themes, and subjects.

Copy – Manuscript pages before being set in type.

Copy editing – The line by line editing of a manuscript.

Copyright – The lawful protection of a writer's work and considered to be in effect at the time of writing or by recording.

Cover letter – A one page, or brief letter to an editor sent with a manuscript.

D

Deadline – The date when a writer's work must be ready.

Denouement – The outcome, solution, or unraveling of a plot.

Description – Technique of describing or picturing by way of words.

Dialogue – The passages of talk or conversations in a play or story.

Disk copy – Circular plate on which data is stored; disk copy of a manuscript.

Draft – First or rough copies of a story, article, or other material.

E

Editing – To revise and make ready a manuscript

Editor – A person who's work is procuring and editing manuscripts

E-mail – Mail sent electronically by a computer.

Epiphany ending – The end of a story that gives the reader a sense of understanding and insight.

Exposition – The writing that explains facts, ideas, who characters are, the setting and related information.

F

Fair use – A provision in copyright law that allows the use of short quotes or passages to be used from copyrighted work.

Fiction – A story or other work of the imagination and portraying imaginary characters and events.

First serial rights – The right to publish materials for the first time before it is in book form.

Flashback – Filling in details in a story to let the reader know something that happened in the past. Also called back story

Flash forward – A device in writing that prepares the reader for events to come without going into specific details. Also called foreshadowing.

Free writing – Unrestrained writing that allows ideas to flow. Also called clustering or brainstorming. Methods of generating fresh ideas.

G

Galleys – The first set of proofs of a manuscript before being prepared in page form.

Genré – A category or type of fiction: Horror, western, romance, science fiction, etc....

H

Hard copy – A copy of a manuscript printed from a computer.

Hook – The lead into a story that keeps the reader interested. To hook or grab interest.

37

I

Imprint – A publisher's line. Example: Jan, an imprint of Robin House Publishers.

J

Juvenile fiction – stories for children ages 2 to 12.

Justify – Printing in line or flush. As when typing a manuscript, you may not want to justify right margins.

L

Lead-in – The beginning of a new scene.

Lead time – The time between planning a book and the publication date.

Literary agent – The person who represents an author, finds a publisher and negotiates contracts.

M

Mainstream – Fiction that has a prevailing and strong trend.

Manuscript – An author's unpublished work in typewritten pages. Abbreviated ms or mss (plural).

Mass market – Books that appeal to a wide readership and are sold in various outlets such as grocery, stationary and drug stores.

Masthead – A list of a magazine's staff members, their titles and departments.

Metaphor – A figure of speech where a word or phrase used for one thing is applied to another as in imagery. Example: A snowfall of white beard covered the old man's face.

Multiple submissions – Submitting more than one story to the same editor at the same time.

N

Narration – The events in a story related by the person telling the story.

Narrator – The person who tells a story.

O

One-time rights – Permission to reprint an author's work one time only.

Opposition – A person who resists, has an opposite stance or contradicts another.

Outline – A summary of a story or book contents.

P

Pace – The slowing down or speeding up of a story by punctuation, dialogue, or the author's style and use of language.

Pen name – Pseudonym an author chooses to use to conceal his or her own name.

Plot – The events scheme or plan of a story through which characters progress.

Premise – A short explanation of what the story is about.

Proofreading – The careful reading and correcting of errors in a manuscript using proofreader's marks.

Proposal – An offer to write a specific work.

Protagonist – The lead character in a story; the hero.

Public domain – Written material that is no longer copyrighted or has never been copyrighted.

Q

Query letter (a letter of inquiry) – A type of cover letter, usually one page, written to an editor in which the writer proposes a story, book, article, or an idea to the editor.

R

Rejection slip – A note from a publishing house that accompanies the return or refusal of an author's work.

Reprint rights – The right of a publisher to print an article or other work after it has been printed by another publication.

Resolution – The solution to a problem. A decision for future action. The end of a story made clear by an explanation.

Revision – To read carefully and correct, improve, update, or change a manuscript or other writing.

Royalties – A specified percentage paid for the work of an author.

S

SASE – Self addressed stamped envelope sent by an author for the return of work not accepted for publication.

Setting – The time period and location in which a story takes place.

Simultaneous submissions – Sending copies of a manuscript to more than one publisher at the time.

Simile – A figure of speech in which one thing is likened to another. Example: "A river of tears" or "Tears flowed like a river."

Slant – Writing a topic with a different approach.

Slush-pile – The stack of unsolicited manuscripts not likely to be accepted by a publisher.

Subplot – The secondary story running thread-like through the main plot.

Subsidiary rights – All the rights in addition to or other than book rights a published author may agree upon.

Synopsis – A brief summary of a story, usually a page or two, written to interest the editor in the complete work.

T

Tag – The words following the quoted dialogue of a character. Example: "Where are you?" he asked. "I am at the store," she said.

Theme – The central and dominant idea of a story or other work, also called the backbone, the message, or main thread.

Tone – The manner of writing that shows the attitude of the narrator.

Transition – A word, phrase, sentence, or paragraph that relates a preceding topic to a succeeding one. The connecting of one idea to the next.

U

Unsolicited submissions – Manuscripts sent to a publisher without an agency representation or that an editor did not ask to see.

V

Viewpoint – The position from which the narrator tells the story and how the story's action is meant to be seen by the reader.

AUTHORS BIOGRAPHIES

Francine Barish-Stern has been an author for over 40 years, and has received numerous awards for poetry and short stories. Her "Rainbow City" won first place and was published in "The Arts Newspaper." She has been a writer for newspapers and magazines and has worked on over 18 books including, "TELL IT TO THE FUTURE" and "NEW HORIZONS." She has recently finished her first full length novel "Code 47 to B R EV Force." Francine has developed writing programs for all ages and has created and designed materials for numerous businesses. She teaches writing, acting and co-wrote and produced, the play, "The WE Nobody Knows" for Crown Players. Also an accomplished business writer, she has specialized in seminars on telemarketing. Francine has recently added photography to her creative interests and has won major awards for her exhibits. Recently, her photograph, "Falls at the Bridge" was exhibited at the Art Museum of Western Virginia. All her art work are produced exclusively as Art on Gold and can be seen at Creations in Roanoke Virginia. .

Bobbi R. Madry, Educational Director for The Write Source and Golden Quill Press also serves as consultant, author and editor. During her career which has spanned more than 50 years, she has also served as senior editor of numerous books and educational publications for major New York City publishers. She has also written book reviews for national magazines. Bobbi served as Associate Publisher for a New York newspaper where she also mentored aspiring writers. She has received numerous awards for writing and community service. Bobbi teaches writing and poetry and holds degrees in the Arts and Behavioral Sciences. Her published works: Human Relations For Business - A Vocational Dictionary - The Job Seeker's Guide - Love Makes The Difference - Work Force 2000 (co-author) - The Professional Models Handbook (co-author). She has been the co-author and editor for Tell it to the Future and New Horizons as well editor of over 18 books published by Golden Quill Press, and is presently authoring several new books.

Books By Golden Quill Press

CODE 47 to BREV Force
By: F.Barish-Stern

The adventures of The BREV Force: College Students fighting to defeat the evils of Controller, a renegade computer virus, threatening to take over the world

TELL IT TO THE FUTURE
BY: Francine R. Cefola (F.Barish-Stern)   & Bobbi R. Madry

TELL IT TO THE FUTURE-Have I Got A Story For You ... about the Twentieth Century leaves personal messages with timelines and stories about our hopes, dreams, or events that impacted on, or changed our lives. Each story focuses on events from a specific decade of the twentieth century with descriptions that reflect the color of the times. Some are witty, some filled with wisdom, while others pull at your heart strings.

LOVE MAKES A DIFFERENCE -
BY: Mary Bianchini and Bobbi Madry

Arriving as an immigrant with her mother in the early 1900's, Mary grew up to become one of the most influential figures in Rockland County, N.Y. Honored by four Presidents and in the Congressional Record, Mary shares her advice about family, community service and reaching her dreams.

NEW HORIZONS -
Life's Poetic Connections
BY: Francine R. Cefola (F. Barish-Stern)
& Bobbi R. Madry

Poetry is the art that speaks to our hearts and minds. Like a beautiful painting or a musical composition, this collection of poetry will take you into worlds limited only by your imagination... from the splendor of a sunset to tasting candy, to memories from a rocking chair ... **Let These Poems Take You To Your Own New Horizons!!**

CHALLENGING MESSAGES
FROM BEYOND

BY: Marjorie Struck

Does the Spiritual World have a message for us? Can we learn to understand that communication? Marjorie Struck certainly believes. This is her personal story of how a message form Beyond changed her life. Informative, at times shocking, but ultimately a journey that reveals a side of the spiritual world that can transform you-forever. Marjorie invites you along to witness how this revelation helped her understand the connection between life and beyond-and how souls in the after life help us to find the Light!

COMPASSION'S LURE

BY: Kathleen Lukens

This is the story of a visionary. Kathy Lukens founder of Camp Venture - advocate for all people with special needs stood up for the rights and deeds of those who could not fight for themselves. With words backed by tireless efforts, Kathy made the impossible happen for the developmentally disabled- a home and the proper attention to their needs. She was truly one of the Great Women of our times.

the GRANPA SPIDER stories

BY: Granpa Spider

A delightful story for children of all ages. Granpa Spider weaves a web of adventure and intrigue, mystery and fun! Along with his Arachnid friends, Penelope, The Colonel,   and others we journey into the exciting world of the web. As Shamrock McGee says, "May the wind be at your web. May your web be in the trees. May cicada be chattering. May there be a host of bees, And, may the web that you spin be serving all your needs... "

MAE SINGS
ABOUT SHORT VOWELS

BY: Karen A. Coleman

"Mae Sings About Short Vowels," was developed by Karen Coleman, as a method for teaching music, while learning vowel sounds. The book uses songs and a vowel recognition technique in an interactive way to help students improve reading skills while learning musical notes

OPENING THE DOOR
TO A BRIGHTER FUTURE

BY: Daniel Windheim

After writing and publishing," It's Not All Black And White" which dealt with the experiences of my son, Dan ,sustaining a traumatic brain injury and the efforts he made to recover and build a productive life, we decided that many of the lessons both Dan and I learned from that experience might have relevance to others recovering from injuries or illnesses. We therefore set out to write a book detailing ten key strategies that could help individuals in their recovery efforts and to share the experiences of some survivors as they struggle to return to a healthy life. As Dan notes'" There is not time to waste focusing on the negative, but we need to take what we have and make the most out of things."

THE POEM BOOK

BY: Daniel Windheim

A brain injury victim of a car accident young Daniel Windheim's life is turned upside down. He turns to poetry to express his frustration, anger and and to take the reader on a beautiful journey through recuperation and new life challenges. Daniel Windheim is truly a shining hero, overcoming life's worst experience. "I remain practical; but a realist, and accept what I am. Life is good, and there is goodness in life."

SWEET MERCY

BY: Rebecca H. Cofer

Katherine Ryder peels away the decades of family secrets to tell her story of growing up in Fairburn, Georgia at the turn of the century - 1900. She battles many obstacles to free herself from small town life and her autocratic mother and moves to Atlanta. In the big city she is betrayed by the man she loves. But her generous heart and hard work pay off, bringing her joy and fulfillment in the end.

THERE IS HOPE

BY: Debby Paine

There Is Hope is a collection of religious poetry about the struggles, pains questions and fears we all face. Debby's love of family, church and community is portrayed as she searches for and reaches toward God to find hope. These poems from the heart-for the heart, will reach out to everyone searching for hope. " Reach for it. Hold on to it. 'Hope is There.' "

Other books marketed by Golden Quill Press:

YOU ARE WHAT YOU WEAR

BY:William Thourlby

"First impressions" are lasting. YOU ARE WHAT YOU WEAR will help you make the right "first impression." Develop skills that are cost effective because they not only increase the quality of life in the workplace, contribute to employee morale and embellish the company image, they play a major role in developing a person's self image and generating profits. The lack of these skills can be highly visible and costly for any person or company in every day and age.

PASSPORT TO POWER

BY: William Thourlby

Part practical, part primer, part visionary, Passport to Power, gives the reader background and formulas to follow to acquire and master international communication skills and provide the keys to unlocking human potential for success as a leader in the new global village of today.

TELL IT TO THE FUTURE

Have I got A Story For You…
About the Twentieth Century

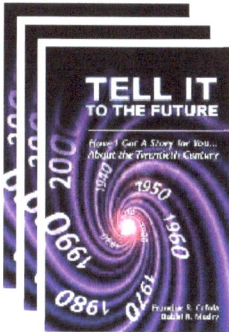
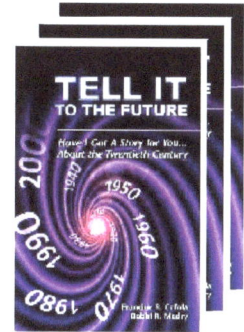

Stories to make

You laugh, Stories to make

You cry

Stories to bring

Back memories of a Time Gone By

Stories of a time that

Most of us never knew

Coming to America…

Going off to war

Just to name a few

These stories vividly paint a portrait of America during the decades

Of the 20th Century…

Am America you'll never forget

GREAT REFERENCE and RESOURCE Book

For the Twentieth Century

BE SURE YOU

TELL IT TO THE FUTURE

Order at www.goldenquillpress.com

www.ingramcontent.com/pod-product-compliance
Lightning Source LLC
Chambersburg PA
CBHW042059040426
42448CB00002B/64